reading aids series

READING AND
THE BILINGUAL CHILD

Doris C. Ching
California State University at Los Angeles

Review Editor   Helen J. James

an service bulletin

international reading association • newark delaware 19711

INTERNATIONAL READING ASSOCIATION

Copyright 1976 by the
International Reading Association, Inc.

Library of Congress Cataloging in Publication Data
Ching, Doris C   1930–
    Reading and the bilingual child.

    (Reading aids series) (An IRA service bulletin)
    Bibliography: p.
    1. Education, Bilingual—United States.
2. Reading—United States.   3. English language—
Study and teaching—United States.   I. Title.
LC3731.C55   371.9'7   76-11800
ISBN 0-87207-220-7

Fourth Printing, December 1983

CONTENTS

FOREWORD

Over the years, the basic aim of the *Reading Aids Series* has been to provide classroom teachers with practical teaching suggestions in specialized subject areas. *Reading and the Bilingual Child* is an important addition to the Series and successfully contributes to the growing demand for materials in the area of bilingual education. Consequently, this title should prove to be a valuable resource for both classroom teachers and tutors of the bilingual child.

Doris Ching's vast experience working with bilingual students and her numerous publications on the topic eminently qualify her to provide educators not only with practical teaching suggestions for the bilingual student, but with an authoritative and succinct summary of the research from which teaching methods have been generated.

The content of *Reading and the Bilingual Child* is well-organized and progresses in a logical manner. The discussion begins with a description of the bilingual child's special needs with regard to preservation of his own cultural values, self-concept, and language, followed by the exposition of four approaches which have received much attention in the literature concerned with teaching English as a second language. Teaching strategies are provided for developing language and concepts, followed by a discussion of the considerations involved in selecting a formal reading approach for use with bilingual children.

Classroom teachers will continue to be faced with the challenge of teaching reading to children with unique and special needs. Those who turn to this publication will profit from the clear exposition of the material it contains. It should become a primary resource handbook for educators of bilingual children.

Thomas C. Barrett, *President*
International Reading Association
1975–1976

INTRODUCTION

Reading and the Bilingual Child is designed for teachers, as well as student teachers, of bilingual (including bidialectal) children. This volume presents a wealth of practical teaching techniques and strategies which are applicable in every classroom. It is authoritatively written and includes these important features:

- Describes the special needs of the bilingual child to help the teacher better identify and understand the child's specific learning needs.

- Reviews and summarizes research on teaching English as a second language and shows the various teaching approaches used in meeting the reading needs of bilingual children.

- Provides a wealth of practical ideas for the classroom teacher in the reading instruction of the bilingual child, with suggestions for the development of motivation and self-concept, auditory discrimination, vocabulary and concepts, oral language, and formal reading instruction.

nult

Chapter 1

THE BILINGUAL CHILD

● Who Is the Bilingual Child?

The problems of the bilingual* child continue to be of interest and concern to educators. Bilingualism is still prevalent in the United States in the large metropolitan areas, in the rural areas of the Midwest and South, in the five southwestern states, and in Hawaii. In some areas, bilinguals constitute all or nearly all of the school population, for example, the Puerto Rican districts in New York City; the Chicano (Mexican-American) sections in cities of the Southwest; and the Chinatown areas of New York City, San Francisco, and Los Angeles.

When the term *bilingualism* is used, there is frequently a vagueness of meaning attached to it. Some people think of a bilingual as an equilingual, a person who can perform proficiently in all aspects of both languages. However, when bilingualism is used in its broadest sense, it is considered without qualification as to the degree of difference between the two languages or systems known; it is immaterial whether the two systems are *languages, dialects of the same language,* or *varieties of the same dialect.* Thus, a bilingual's achievement may be limited to one aspect of a language, dialect, or variety of a dialect, such as understanding, speaking, reading, writing; or he may have varying degrees of ability in all these aspects. Actually, bilingualism and monolingualism can be thought of as opposite extremes of a continuum, with a continuum for each aspect of language, dialect, or variety of a dialect (*33*).

The teacher in a classroom of bilinguals is likely to encounter children who show great variety in their patterns of linguistic competency. Some may speak very little English while others may speak English almost as well as their mother tongue. In some

*Some linguists prefer to keep the labels *bilingual* and *bidialectal* separate and distinct, using bilingual to describe those who speak two languages and bidialectal to describe those who speak two dialects of a language. However, the writer is in agreement with those linguists who feel that bilingual includes bidialectal learners, and this is the manner in which the term is used in this book.

1

instances, the child may actually be a monolingual, understanding and speaking only his mother tongue (such as Spanish or Chinese) when he enters school where English is the medium of instruction. In ghetto urban centers of large metropolitan cities there is concern for the Black child who may use a nonstandard or variant dialect containing consistent and regular deviations from standard English dialect forms. Since standard English is the dialect accepted by the majority in the United States because of the social and political positions of the people who speak it, the public unfortunately regards those who speak nonstandard dialects as uneducated persons and holds them in low esteem when, in fact, use of the nonstandard dialect simply indicates that the speaker was reared in a language environment in which that particular dialect was spoken. Teachers who work with bilingual children are thus often confronted with children who have special needs in the school situation.

- **Special Needs of the Bilingual Child**

There are a number of special needs and learning problems which the teacher must be aware of if he is to effectively guide bilingual children toward successful school achievement.

1. *Cultural Values*

It is especially important that the teacher of bilingual children develop sensitivities to the cultural values of the children he teaches. As Zintz (*37*) so aptly states:

> Too many teachers are inadequately prepared to understand or accept these dissimilar cultural values. Teachers come from homes where the drive for success and achievement has been internalized early, where "work for work's sake" is rewarded, and where time and energy are spent building for the future. Many children come to the classroom with a set of values and background of experiences radically different from that of the average American child. To teach these children successfully, the teacher must be cognizant of these differences and must above all else seek to understand without disparagement those ideas, values, and practices different from his own.

The following are significant areas to be considered by the teacher in working with bilingual children:

Level of aspiration. Progress in learning in the school situation is contingent upon goal setting which is both challenging and realistic. The child should be helped to set goals which are within his grasp but which are also rewarding in terms of effortful achievement. This goal setting orientation may be lacking in the child if he has had little experience with success, has a vague sense of futurity, and has come to feel that he is powerless to command any control over his destiny.

Value orientation. Certain fairly standard values that are held by the general society may not be values held by the child in his culture.

For example, because he may lack such values as respect for personal and property rights of others, common courtesy, citizenship responsibilities, intrafamilial duties, and appropriate regard for authority, he may encounter derision and rejection from his peers.

Socialization. Children may come from environments in which the practical social amenities necessary for harmonious interaction with others or for appropriate behavior in school have not been acquired. It is the responsibility of the teacher to help children develop social skills which may include sharing, taking turns, respect for the classroom authority figure, and various forms of self-control which are fundamental to socialization.

The teacher of children with these needs must be open minded; he must not approach children with misconceptions and prejudices. He must accept the children as they are and make them feel worthy as individuals. He must become acquainted with the children's cultures and understand and accept them. He must have no prejudices against race or socioeconomic levels and must not consider his values to be the "best." Knowing how he acquired his own set of values, the teacher must help these children to develop values of their own without negatively affecting their self-concepts in the process.

The teacher of bilingual children should change cultural differences into cultural advantages. The various ethnic groups and cultures provide numerous resources which can be used to enrich classroom learning.

2. *Sense of Personal Worth*

The teacher of bilingual children must provide them with a program which gives them opportunities to feel secure, to feel accepted, to receive peer recognition, and to achieve success in learning. The teacher can assist in developing children's ego strengths through encouragement and sincere praise. It is especially important that he maintain a happy, relaxed school atmosphere—one in which children are free to converse, to enjoy and share experiences, to use language, and to make mistakes and correct them. If a child speaks a language other than Engligh or a nonstandard dialect of English at home, the teacher should be accepting of the language or dialect with which the child is most familiar. The teacher should help the child see that his language is accepted and that he may continue to use it with his family and friends. A child is quick to sense teacher rejection of his language. Such rejection by the teacher can only serve as a barrier to communication between teacher and pupil. Along with the acceptance of the child's language, however, it is important for the teacher to help the child see that he must learn to use standard English in certain situations. The teacher who approaches the use of the languages or dialects in this way will find children with attitudes more conducive to learning to use standard English.

3

The teacher of such children must beware of conveying an expectation of low achievement. It is crucial that children view with optimism their probability of success in learning as well as eventual achievement of life's goals. Many learning situations in which they experience success are essential for these children if they are to develop healthy self-images rather than defeatist attitudes which frequently account for failure and for their holding low levels of aspiration for themselves.

3. *Language*

Before bilingual children can learn to read English, they must be able to understand and speak it effectively. Frequently, teachers push children into reading before they can understand English well and speak it fluently. It is no wonder bilingual children encounter difficulty and eventual failure in learning to read and thus develop negative attitudes toward reading. Following are possible language needs of bilingual children which must be developed before they are taught to read:

Experiential-conceptual-informational background. Many bilingual children fail to comprehend what they read in the school situation because they lack the vital first-hand experiences necessary to expand their fund of concepts and general information and because they have experienced the life adventures of their own particular cultures which are not represented in the school texts.

Reading ability is negatively affected by meagre backgrounds of experience, concepts, and general information. Although a child may be able to recognize words on the printed page, the words will be meaningless nonsense if the child does not know what concepts they represent. Thus, the teacher of bilingual children must provide an educational program containing a variety of experiences and the mediation essential to help children acquire meaningful concepts.

Auditory discrimination. Because bilingual children have been exposed to a system of speech sounds which is at considerable variance with the standard regional dialects of American English, they may have difficulty in comprehending the speech of others and may pronounce English words incorrectly in their own speech. The results of a study by Tireman (28) of the vocabulary of Spanish speaking children showed that phonetic interference caused by differences in the phonemic structure of English and Spanish was cause for many errors in pronunciation and meaning of English words. For example, when the word being tested was *hit,* children would give the long *e* sound to the short *i* sound. This response then sounded like *heat,* and the children would speak of the "heat of the stove" when using the word in a sentence.

Auditory discrimination ability correlates significantly with success in learning to read, as children must be familiar with speech sounds before they can master the symbols used to represent them on the printed page. Inadequately developed auditory discrimination undoubtedly accounts for much of the difficulty bilingual children experience with phonics in learning to read.

Bilingual children lacking in auditory discrimination ability are penalized in listening situations. Because much learning takes place through listening in the school situation, if words are misperceived or confused with similar sounding words, there is likely to be inaccurate listening comprehension which leads to difficulties in the learning process in the school situation. Thus, bilingual children must be immersed in the speech sounds they are to acquire. They must be given opportunities to imitate adequate speech models and be assisted when speech sounds are not perceived or pronounced correctly.

Vocabulary development. The bilingual child's vocabulary may be inadequate because concepts which he has developed may have labels or names which are unique within his own culture. For example, when the Black child asks, "Will you *carry* me to school?" he means "Will you *take* me to school?" When his mother asks the child to *crank* the window, she is asking him to *open* the window. When the father tells the child to stop *meddling,* he is telling him to stop *fighting.* The child may have no names or labels at all for certain concepts since he has not had opportunities to communicate about them with anyone. For example, when the child enters kindergarten he may not know the names of the various parts of his body because he has not talked about them with anyone at home. In homes where both English and another language are spoken, the child may have learned the Chinese or Spanish word for a concept rather than the English word and thus be handicapped when he is confronted with unfamiliar words in the English language. Therefore, the bilingual child who has a restricted English vocabulary must be provided with a variety of meaningful experiences where new English words and their meanings are communicated with clarity and precision.

Syntax. The syntactical structure with which the bilingual child is familiar is frequently quite at variance with that which he hears or tries to read in school. Both the word order and the degree of complexity of sentences in textbooks and which the teacher uses in the classroom are likely to overwhelm the child. To help the child acquire the patterns of speech of the English language, the teacher must provide many opportunities for him to hear and use English in various situations such as listening to stories, singing songs, memorizing poems or lines from plays, and participating in choral reading *(7).*

From the foregoing, it is evident that when the bilingual child enters school he may encounter many problems and difficulties if the curriculum is not adapted to his needs. If the teacher is not aware of the language deficiencies and special needs the child may have because of his environmental background, the child may have few successful and rewarding experiences and develop generalized frustrations and negative feelings about school. Of course, not all the negative factors and deficits discussed here are present in every bilingual child. They may be present in varying degrees or not be present at all. It is important, however, that the teacher of such children have a knowledge and understanding of their home environments, and of the language deficiencies and needs that may result, so that he can adapt the curriculum to individual student needs and develop those skills which will make the child's school experience stimulating and rewarding.

- **Appraisal of the Bilingual Child's Needs**

Appraisal of the bilingual child's linguistic and reading skills should be made before a program of instruction is planned and devised. The teacher should also gather information about the child's cultural background and his background of knowledge and experience, amount of previous schooling, attitude toward learning in the school situation, and sense of personal worth. This may be done through observing and talking with the child, keeping anecdotal records, and visiting the child's home and getting acquainted with his parents (13).

A recorder should be used to tape the child's speech so that his individual linguistic needs may be analyzed. If standardized tests (such as readiness tests) are utilized for diagnostic purposes, they should be used selectively with the understanding that certain items in the tests may exhibit cultural, social, or linguistic bias and the results may not reflect a true indication of the child's potential and ability. However, the tests may indicate to the teacher some of the needs of the child and the experiences which must be provided before the child is ready for formal reading instruction.

Bilingual tests that may be used in appraising the needs and abilities of the bilingual child are the Cooperative Inter-American Tests published by the Educational Testing Service, Princeton, New Jersey. These tests are comprised of sets of comparable tests in English and Spanish and, therefore, measure the same reading skills in the two languages.

It is important that the teacher acquire a basic knowledge of the sound and structure of the child's first language so that he may be aware of the linguistic divergencies between the child's first language and standard English and the possible interferences in sound and structure. Acquisition of this knowledge could help the teacher understand the difficulties being experienced so that he may guide the child more effectively.

Chapter 2

RESEARCH ON TEACHING ENGLISH AS A SECOND LANGUAGE AND READING

Year after year in the United States, thousands of bilingual children encounter frustration and failure in learning to read standard English. Various studies have endeavored to find the most effective approaches for helping bilingual children learn to read successfully. Venezky (30) has reviewed and summarized some of these findings and results. He found that there are four main approaches used in the studies: 1) native literacy approach, 2) dialect approach, 3) standard language approach, and 4) common core approach.

● **Native Literacy Approach**

The native literacy approach is based upon the assumption that the most efficient method for teaching the national language of a country to nonspeakers of that language is to teach literacy first in the native language, then (or simultaneously with the teaching of reading in the first language) teach the national language orally, and finally teach reading in the national language.

The native literacy approach is theoretically and logically appealing because: 1) by teaching reading in the native language, reading instruction can begin at an earlier age than if the standard language has to be taught first; 2) the child's cultural heritage is recognized and honored; and 3) learning to read is undertaken in the language with which the child is most comfortable.

However, native literacy programs are expensive; they require not only the development of new reading materials but the training of special teachers and the design of testing materials which are valid for the languages concerned. In the United States, we are still working to develop and improve reading and testing materials which are valid for standard English. To attempt to repeat this process for all languages spoken natively within the United States would require tremendous expenditures in excess of what can be realistically acquired.

Experiments which compare the native literacy approach with the standard language approach have been carried out in the Philippines *(18)*; in San Antonio, Texas *(11)*; and in Mexico *(16)*. None of these major studies shows unequivocally superior results for the native literacy approach. In the sixth and final year of the Philippines experiment, there was no statistical difference between the groups for reading ability. In the 1967 report of the San Antonio Project, no increase in reading ability was found in the native literacy group over that resulting from the control groups which received standard teaching methods. In the Modiano study, where reading instruction in the native languages in the Highlands of Mexico was claimed to be superior to that in the national language (Spanish), neither the schools nor the teachers' backgrounds were equivalent, and they were probably more important factors than the teaching methods. In summary, although the native literacy approach possesses obvious cultural advantages over the standard language approach, it has yet to be proven scholastically superior.

● **The Dialect Approach**

The dialect approach is one in which the child first learns to read in the nonstandard dialect with which he enters school. Its primary merit is that the child will receive "powerful egosupport" through the credence given to his language *(6)*. The negative aspects of this approach are: 1) the difficulty of preparing special materials for each dialect group in the United States (Southern regional white, Appalachian, Northern urban Negro, American Indian, Hawaiian pidgin, Mexican-American, Cuban derived Spanish-American, Southern Negro) and not just reading materials but, according to Baratz and Shuy *(6)*, "transitional readers" that would aid the child in changing from vernacular texts to standard English texts; and 2) according to Goodman *(9)*, who has been involved with the teaching of reading to Black children in innercity Detroit, "parents and leaders in the speech community . . . would reject the use of special materials which are based on a non-prestigious dialect. They usually share the view of the general culture that their speech is not the speech of cultivation and literature." In integrated classrooms, each child would have the reading materials which most closely match his language and environment. This would make group instruction very difficult for the classroom teacher.

Most of the evidence indicates that dialect differences per se are not major barriers to learning to read. Studies done by Peisach *(20)*, Weener *(32)*, and Eisenberg et al. *(8)*, indicate that lower socioeconomic Black children do not find standard English any less intelligible than Black speech (educated or uneducated).

● The Standard Language Approach

The standard language approach is one in which teaching English as a second language or dialect is the first step in teaching reading, as opposed to teaching standard English as the only language or dialect. This approach has been advocated by some because it is felt that it is easier to start English as a second language in the kindergarten or earlier.

It must also be recognized that if the entire reading situation is to be familiar and comfortable for the child, then not just standard English language but some standard English culture must be taught. This might delay the teaching of reading for a semester or even a year. However, if this procedure does improve the teaching of reading to nonstandard speakers, its advocates feel that the results achieved are worth the time spent.

Recent projects for teaching English as a second language include one being carried on in Chaflin, North Carolina, and another in Wakulla County, Florida. Although it is too early to draw any definite conclusions about the programs, their initial successes are encouraging.

● The Common Core Approach

In the common core approach, materials which minimize dialect and cultural differences are developed in standard English. To minimize dialect differences requires careful comparisons of standard English with the major nonstandard dialects. This task has already been undertaken for northern Black speech. Shuy *(23)* lists only three syntactic forms which require special attention for cross dialectal materials: negation (*doesn't have* versus *ain't got no*), past conditional questions (*Mother asked if I ate* versus *Mother asked did I eat*), and negative + be (*When I sing he isn't afraid* versus *When I sing he don't be afraid*).

An effective means for minimizing cultural differences is to base the content of the reading materials upon a school subject such as science (this is being done in the San Antonio Project) or civics, which the children learn together as common experiences in the school situation.

At this time, research studies show that there is no conclusive evidence that one approach is superior to another. It is recognized, however, that standard English reading materials should be introduced at some point in the school situation. Venezky *(30)* suggests that such reading materials be used under the following conditions:

1. Children whose dialects deviate markedly from standard English should be taught the standard dialect before they are taught read-

ing with standard English materials. However, standard English should be considered as a second dialect and not as the correct dialect.

2. Reading materials should be as dialect free and culture free as possible in content, vocabulary, and syntax.

3. Allow the child, regardless of his own dialect, to translate from standard written English to his own speech; that is, dialect differences should not be considered reading errors.

Chapter 3

TEACHING STRATEGIES FOR READING INSTRUCTION
OF THE BILINGUAL CHILD

Following are suggested strategies for developing the reading skills of bilingual children. Many of these practices have been used by teachers of bilingual children, and they have proved to be valuable in the development of reading skills.

In using the various suggested practices in the reading instruction of the bilingual child, the teacher should integrate the language activities into her whole school program as language is the vehicle of all instruction in every aspect of the school day. Only then will the English language skills of the bilingual child be developed and internalized so that he may learn to read English without encountering difficulties and feelings of frustration and failure.

● **Development of Motivation and Self-Concept**

The needs of the bilingual child that must be met first by the teacher are those of increasing his motivation to learn in the school situation and enhancing his self-concept. The following strategies may be utilized to accomplish these goals:

1. Develop a bond of trust and friendship between teacher and pupil. The child who trusts and likes his teacher will learn to respect his teacher and will want to win his approval. To develop this bond of trust and friendship, the teacher must show the child through actions and words that he likes him, respects him and his cultural background, accepts his language, believes in him, and expects him to succeed in learning activities selected to meet his needs within the school situation.

2. Provide an atmosphere which will encourage the child to share his home and daily experiences and to talk about himself, his personal interests, and his aspirations. Until the child gains confidence and ease in speaking in the classroom situation, do not make comments such as "Speak loudly so everyone can hear you" or "Pronounce your words more clearly" or "Look at your audience when you are speaking."

3. Provide books in the classroom library and display pictures and various artifacts relating to the cultural heritage of the child in order to reinforce self-identification.

4. Use a camera (Polaroid, if possible) to take photos of class activities and to photograph individual pupils. Then use the photos to motivate oral, writing, and reading activities. Of course, this will also be helpful in development of positive self-concept.

5. Provide live models of achievement by having men and women of the child's cultural background, who have succeeded in various lines of endeavor, speak to the class. The speakers may give biographical details and tell something about their jobs. After the talks, give the children the opportunity to ask questions (24). The diverse careers of the models may help to raise the children's aspirations concerning their own careers.

6. Develop a unit of study relating to the cultural heritages of the bilingual children. Have them bring to class and share materials they may have, such as collections of stamps or coins of the country being studied, artifacts or handicraft of the country's artisans, or various types of clothing worn by people of the country. The unit of study should include the art, music, dance, and literature of the culture. Such a unit of study in the classroom will provide many opportunities for bilingual children to be recognized by their peers.

7. Give bilingual children many opportunities to be recognized by their peers, not only through sharing but also through academic accomplishments. Also help the children develop leadership abilities by initially providing situations in which they might be chairpersons of committees or be responsible for seeing that tasks are carried out by small groups. As abilities to lead increase, responsibilities may be enlarged. Such responsibilities will afford recognition which will enhance self-concept.

8. Involve parents and siblings in class activities whenever possible; for example, invite parents to share their knowledge and materials relating to their culture and ask siblings to share their hobbies or personal interests with the children. Such activities among the children will develop pride in one's own family and will enhance the self-concepts of the participants.

● **Language Development**

Bilingual children will be able to succeed in learning to read English only when they have developed good listening and speaking abilities in the English language. Teachers of bilingual children must not begin formal reading instruction of English until the children have acquired adequate English language skills; otherwise, the children may be doomed to frustration and failure in learning to read.

Before the teacher begins developing the standard English language skills of the bilingual child, he should be aware of the points of linguistic interferences and conflicts in sound and structure between the child's first language and standard English. Following are points of conflict between standard English and the phonological and grammatical aspects of Spanish, Chinese, and Black English.

Summary of Phonological and Grammatical Variations in English and Spanish (22)

1. Certain vowel sounds will be difficult for the Spanish speaking child: /I/ bit; /æ/ bat; /ə/ but; and /u/ full.

2. English relies on voiced (vocal cords vibrate) and voiceless (vocal cords do not vibrate) sounds to establish meaning contrasts, but Spanish does not: bit-pit; buzz-bus.

3. The Spanish speaker does not use these sounds in his language: /v/ vote; /ð/ then; /z/ zoo; /ž/ measure; /ĵ/ jump. Often the speaker will replace these sounds with sounds he perceives to closely resemble them, or with sounds that frequently occur in similar positions in Spanish.

4. Words that end in /r/ plus the consonants /d, t, l, p/ and /s/ are pronounced without the final consonant: card-car, cart-car.

5. In Spanish the blend of /s/ and the consonant sounds /t, p, k, f, m, n, l/ does not occur, nor does any Spanish word begin with the /s/ + consonant sound. A vowel sound precedes the /s/, and the consonant that follows begins the second syllable of the word. Thus the child has the problem not only of starting the word with the /s/, but also of pronouncing two consonants (star may thus become estar and be pronounced es-tar). The final consonant clusters /sp/ wasp, /sk/ disk, and /st/ last also present problems in consonant pronunciation.

6. Grammatical differences between the two systems may include the following: subject-predicate agreement (The cars runs.); verb tense (I need help yesterday.); use of negative forms (He no go home.); omission of noun determiner in certain contexts (He is farmer.); omission of pronoun forms (Is farmer?); order of adjectives (The cap red is pretty.); and comparison (Is more big.).

This summary serves only as an introduction to the teacher to help him in being alert to the variations between the Spanish and English languages.

Summary of Phonological and Grammatical Variations in English and Chinese (22)

There are many dialects of Chinese with Mandarin, which is spoken by approximately 70 percent of the Chinese people as the national dialect. Cantonese, another major dialect, is spoken by most of the Chinese families that come to the United States from Hong Kong, Kowloon, or Macao. Thus, the Cantonese dialect is the one that is discussed below.

1. English has many more vowels than Chinese; for example, /ay/ buy; /aw/ bough; /ɔ/ bought. There is specific difficulty with production of certain vowels such as the front vowels /iy/ beat, /ey/ bait. This results in homophones for a significant number of English words: beat-bit; Luke-look, bait-bet.

2. A number of English consonant sounds are not in Chinese: /θ/ than /ð/ that; /š/ she; /n/ need; and /r/ rice.

3. Many English words end in consonants, but in Chinese many of the consonants are not used in final positions; for example, /f/ is used only initially in Chinese, and the student has difficulty producing it in a final position. Often an extra syllable will be made of the final /f/; day off becomes day offu.

4. Consonant clusters are nonexistent in Cantonese. Those which occur at the ends of words present difficulty in forming plurals and past tenses using /s, t, d, z/: cap-caps, laugh-laughed, wish-wished, dog-dogs.

5. Most grammatical relationships are indicated by word order and auxiliary words in Chinese: "He gave me two books" becomes "Yesterday he give I two book."

6. Numerical designations or auxiliary words are used to indicate plural forms in Chinese: "two books" is "two book."

7. A time word or phrase indicates the tense of a verb. An action verb followed by the auxiliary word *jaw* indicates past or completed tense: "He go jaw" means "He went."

8. Several English word classes—articles, prepositions, and some conjunctions—are reduced or absent in Chinese.

9. The question form in Chinese does not invert the noun and verb forms. Instead, the order is similar to the statement form but the "empty" words *ma* or *la* are added to the end. For example, "Are you an American?" is "You are American ma?" in Chinese.

10. A subject and a predicate are not required in Chinese when the context is sufficient for understanding. For example, "It rains" may be represented as "Drop rain" in Chinese, while "The mountain is big" may be stated as "Mountain big" in Chinese.

11. Tone or pitch in Chinese distinguishes word meanings, but in English pitch combines with intonation to convey sentence meaning.

The above is but a brief summary to help the classroom teacher understand a number of basic difficulties encountered by Chinese youngsters who speak the Cantonese dialect.

Summary of Phonological and Grammatical Variations in Standard English and Black English (34)

Sociolinguists generally suggest that there are more similarities than differences between Black English and standard English. Among the differences, some are more relevant to reading problems than others. The following have been found by Labov *(14)*, Wolfram *(35)*, and Shuy *(23)* to be some of the phonological and grammatical interferences which may affect reading:

1. r-lessness. Black English has a rather high degree of r-lessness. The *r* becomes a schwa or simply disappears before vowels as well as before consonants or pauses: *r* is never pronounced in four, Paris becomes Pass, carrot becomes cat.

2. l-lessness. Dropping of the liquid *l* is similar to that of dropping *r* except that the former is often replaced by a back unrounded glide (u) instead of the center glide for *r*. Or the *l* disappears completely, especially after the backrounded vowels. Examples: help = hep, tool = too, all = awe, fault = fought.

3. Simplification of consonant clusters at the end of words. There is a general tendency to reduce end consonant clusters to single consonants, particularly those ending in /t/, /d/, /s/, or /z/. In approximate order of frequency, the /t,d/ clusters affected are -st, -ft, -nt, -nd, -ld, -zd, -md, thus generating homonyms such as past = pass, meant = men, rift = riff, mend = men, wind = wine, hold = hole. The /s,z/ cluster simplification results in these homonyms: six = sick, box = bock, Max = Mack, mix = Mick. Labiv found that the simplification of the /s,z/ clusters is much more characteristic of Black speakers than of White speakers.

4. Weakening of final consonants. This is another example of a general tendency to produce less information after stressed vowels, so that the endings of words (be they consonants, unstressed final vowels, or weak syllables) are devoiced or dropped entirely. Children who possess this characteristic seem to have the most serious reading problems. Most affected by this are the following: boot = boo, road = row, feed = feet, seat = seed = see, poor = poke = pope, bit = bid = big.

Labov and Wolfram, from their respective studies in Harlem and Detroit, contributed significant data on Black English grammatical rules which may be sources of reading problems.

5. Possessive deletion. The absence of /-s/ inflection results in: John's cousin = John cousin, whoever's book = whoever book. Deletion of /-r/ makes two possessive pronouns identical to personal pronouns: their book = they book, your = you = you-all.

6. Verb suffix. Labov believes that the third person singular was not present in Black English but imported from standard English in view of the low percentage of use (only 5-15 percent in some cases) and

the sharp class stratification between middle and working classes. Some illustrations of the use of the verb suffix in Black English are: Somebody get hurts. He can goes out. He always bes on the beach mosta de time. All our men ares each on side. We goes to church on Sunday. Judy go to school today.

7. Be$_2$ form. There are two forms of "do" and two forms of "have" in English as in "Does he do it?" and "Has he had any?" In the first question, they could be called Do$_1$ and Do$_2$. The second form in each class is a normal main verb. *Be* has a main verb Be$_2$ which is like other main verbs. The meaning of Be$_2$ is so versatile that in some instances standard English has no equivalents:

    a) Habitual rather than a temporal or short occurrence. From now on, I don't be playing. He be sad. I be crying. She always be happy. Guys that bes with us.

    b) Repeated occurrence. Wolfram found between 11 to 16 percent of frequency adverbs with Be$_2$, such as hardly, usually, sometimes, always, mostly, all the time.

    c) Single nonrepeated activity in the future. This practice is used in all cases where *will* is possible or where an underlying *will* could be elicited in tag questions or in negatives: Sometime he don't be busy. He be in in a few minutes. I know he will. Sometime he be busy. I know he do.

    d) Deletion of "would." She just be talking, and I wouldn't listen. If he didn't have to go away, he be home.

8. Copulation. Copula deletion is considered basically a phonological process, but it also has strong grammatical constraints which are not random. Deletion may occur with verb following, no vowel preceding, but pronoun preceding. Semantically, deletion occurs most often on short active utterances: Riff eatin. He going. Ricky too old. Jim goin. She real tired. Carol chairman.

9. Person-number agreement.

    a) In Black English, there is person-number agreement for I am, you are, and he is.

    b) There is no third person singular marker, as in most languages around the world. The preferred forms are: He don't. He do. He have. *Does, has,* and *says* are used infrequently.

    c) *Was* is the preferred form for past tense of *be.*

10. Past tense. Phonological conditioning weakens the regular past tense as in the reduction of /t,d/ inflection: passed=pass, missed=miss, fined=fine, picked=pick, loaned=loan, raised=raise.

11. Negative forms and negation. A study of these forms should convince anyone that Black English has rules as other dialects do. In Black English, *ain't* is used as past negative; for example, I told im I ain't pull it; He didn't do nothing much, and I ain't neither. Adults used

didn't more often than *ain't*. Preteens use *ain't* less often than teenagers. *Ain't* is a stigmatized form but has special social meaning to teenagers.

In negation, Black English seems to carry negative concord principles further than nonstandard Anglo English. Examples: Nobody had no bloody nose or nosebleed. I am no strong drinker. She didn't play with none of us. Down there nobody don't know about no club.

This brief summary concerning Black English is by no means complete but should give the classroom teacher an introduction to variations between Black English and standard English that may affect children's learning to read.

When the teacher has acquired a basic knowledge of the linguistic variations between standard English and the children's first language and when he has diagnosed the specific linguistic needs of the children, he is ready to plan and execute an English language skill development program in his class. Following are some suggestions for the program in the areas of: 1) auditory discrimination, 2) vocabulary and concept development, 3) grammar, and 4) oral expression.

Development of Auditory Discrimination

1. The following activities may be used to stimulate children's auditory acuity or sense of hearing and help them become more aware of the sounds which occur around them.

a) Have the pupils list all the sounds they hear on their way to and from school or on the playground. Have them recall all the sounds they can remember hearing on various trips they have taken—to the zoo, dairy, fire station, airport. The teacher might write the sounds on the board as the children name the various sounds.

b) Have the children make individual lists of both the sounds they enjoy and the sounds they find unpleasant.

c) Ask the children to close their eyes. Make sounds with various objects—coins, pins, pencils, paper, scissors, water glass—and have the pupils guess the object used to make each sound.

d) Have the children sit quietly in the classroom for a few minutes and list all the sounds they hear during that period of time—a car passing, a person walking, a dog barking, someone sneezing, a door slamming.

e) Have storytelling in which each pupil contributes a sentence with a sound mentioned in it. After each pupil contributes his sentence, he calls on another pupil to contribute a sentence. The title of the story may be "The Cave of Mysterious Sounds," "A Trip to the Zoo on the Planet Mars," or "The Town of Noisy People." The children may select their own title for the story.

f) Read stories or poems in which there are various sounds—engines, animals, water, wind, rain. Have the pupils repeat the words or phrases used to create the illusions of the sounds.

g) Have the children watch and listen to a sound film. Tell them to be ready to ask questions about the important points of the film after it is shown.

h) Play games that require attentive listening, such as:

Simon says. A child takes the part of Simon and directs the others to do various things, such as "Clap your hands," "Close your eyes," "Raise your right hand." The directive should not be carried out unless it is preceded by "Simon says."

Gossip. The first child whispers a message to the child next to him and each succeeding child whispers what he heard to the next child. At the end, the final message heard is compared to what the first child whispered.

Going to the grocery store. The first child says, "I'm going to the grocery store to buy some eggs." The next child adds an item to be bought at the store and repeats the preceding item. Each succeeding child adds another item to the list and repeats all preceding items.

The games should be played in small groups once the children have learned the procedures for playing.

2. The tape recorder can be used in a variety of activities to develop pupils' auditory perception.

a) Familiar sounds can be recorded and played back for children to guess what produced each sound. The sounds may be made by clapping hands, ringing a doorbell, knocking on a door, sharpening a pencil, washing a glass, starting a car, or walking on concrete pavement.

b) Children's conversation and discussion periods may be recorded. Then they may listen to what they have said and discuss what aspects could be improved in future sessions.

c) Have the children listen to recorded short stories. Ask them to list all action words or descriptive words that added interest to the stories.

d) Have the children listen to the tape recording of a story. Stop the recorder before the story ends and have various pupils tell how they think the story will end. Then play the rest of the recording.

e) Record children's reports about various topics as they share them with class members. Have members of the class tell what they learned from the oral reports of individual children. Then play the recording to see if important points of the reports were remembered.

f) Poetry and stories may be recorded and then played to the children. Questions about the characters, the sequence, and specific incidents may then be asked and discussed with the pupils. On occasion, before the tape is played, the pupils may be asked to listen for specific things.

Listening centers may be set up in elementary classrooms so that listening activities with the tape recorder can be carried on with some privacy and without disturbing other members of the class. A listening center consists of an audio device with eight or more sets of earphones or headphones, each of which can be plugged individually into the listening center to enable the children to hear the tape recordings. Such listening centers may be used by children during free time or while the teacher is doing individual or group work with other members of the class.

3. Storytelling by the teacher or pupils gives children opportunities to listen appreciatively. The teacher should guide the pupils in learning to respond to the stories or poetry by enjoying the plot or reacting to the mood; creating visual images of the action described; and interpreting the feelings, motivations, and behavior of the characters. Activities such as the following will help children to learn to listen more appreciatively and creatively:

a) Have the children do a spontaneous dramatization of a story or poem read to them.

b) Have the children express in pantomime poetry that is read or reread to them.

c) Have the children write or tell original endings to a story that is read to them.

d) Have the children draw pictures for the "television showing" of a story or poem that is read to them.

4. The following activities may be used by the teacher to develop children's abilities to use correct speech sounds in oral expression:

a) Record lists of words with sounds with which the pupils are having difficulty. The recording should give the pupils opportunity to repeat each word after it has been pronounced. The recording should be used only with teacher guidance until pupils can make the sounds correctly. Then pupils may use the tape for independent practice.

b) When the pupils are able to pronounce correctly the words with the sounds with which they had had difficulty, tape record sentences containing many words with the sounds with which the pupils need practice. Again, the tape should be used with teacher guidance until the pupils can make the sounds correctly in sentences; then, it may be used for independent practice.

c) The classroom may have a tape recording activity center. Each day a different activity may be described on a 5 × 8 card. For example, the pupils may be asked to think of five words with a particular sound in them (such as the short *i* sound) and also think of five sentences, each of which contains a word with the same sound. Of course, the sound selected would be one on which the pupils need practice. The teacher should instruct the pupils in how to use the tape recorder. The pupils may go to the center during free time to execute the activity described for the day or week. Each pupil says his name before doing the activity so that the teacher will be able to evaluate the performances of individual pupils.

d) Have the pupils make individual booklets with pictures of words containing specific sounds with which they need practice. For example, if they have a tendency to omit the final *s* sound from words, they may have a page in their booklets devoted to pictures for words with a final *s*. Have the pupils label their pictures and, during their free time, take turns with classmates naming the pictures to gain oral practice with the sounds.

Vocabulary and Concept Development

1. Direct experience is the chief source and means of vocabulary and concept development. It is from the materials of direct experience that the child develops clear and accurate meanings and concepts by sensing the relationship between verbal symbols and experience. Therefore, the child who has a poor speaking vocabulary should be given the opportunity to examine, manipulate, and talk about various materials, including tools, toys, objects, specimens, and models in the classroom.

2. Specific vocabulary lists may be developed by classroom teachers to guide them in building the vocabulary and concepts of bilingual children. The Dolch list of Basic Sight Vocabulary of 220 Words may be used along with lists of foods; animals; parts of the body; types of clothing; words relating to the home, school and neighborhood environments; and other frequently used words such as *hello, excuse me, lunch,* and *shut.*

3. Various methods must be used to help the child become familiar with words and their meanings:

a) The teacher may show an object, name it, and have the pupils repeat its name. This procedure may be included as part of a game. A "surprise box" may contain a number of objects. A child may be called upon to select an object from the box and, as he does so, the teacher names the object selected, the child repeats the name, and then the whole class pronounces it. Eventually, the child and class name the object by using a sentence such as, "I have a red book in my hand" or "This is a red book." At times the child may be asked by the teacher or another pupil to do something with the object. After following the instruction, the child verbalizes his action to the rest of the group. At other times, the child may perform an act of his own thinking and call on another pupil to describe his action. If the child called upon does it accurately, he is given the opportunity to perform an act with the same object and call on another pupil to describe his action. The teacher may permit this procedure to continue until he feels that the pupils have learned to pronounce the word being taught and have gained an understanding of its meaning by seeing it, feeling it, using it, playing with it, hearing it, smelling it, tasting it, or doing any other action that would extend the meaning of the word.

b) Words that cannot be visualized as specific objects may be dramatized with the use of various materials to convey their meanings. For example, verbs and prepositions (such as *walk, eat, in,* and *on*) may be dramatized by the teacher to develop their meanings. For each word, he may dramatize such sentences as: See me *walk* to the door. I like to *eat* apples. I put the ball *in* the box. I put the pencil *on* the table. He should dramatize several sentences for each of the words to be sure the children understand its meaning. After the dramatization of each word, pupils may be called upon to follow specific directions with the word to show their understanding of it. Each child should verbalize his action after the performance of the act. To check on pupil understanding of each word and to extend its meaning, individual pupils or small groups of pupils may dramatize the meaning of each word in various ways of their own and call on specific pupils to verbalize their performances.

c) The teacher may use simple stick figure illustrations, pictures, recordings, slides, films, filmstrips, diagrams, charts, and books to further extend the meaning and understanding of each word. The pupils themselves may be asked to make illustrations for each new word and phrase and put them together into booklet form. This could be used by the teacher as an evaluative device to check pupil understanding of each word.

d) Another technique to check pupil understanding of each word taught is to ask questions requiring answers which would show pupil knowledge or lack of knowledge of the word. Pupils should answer the questions orally in complete

sentences. Questions such as the following may be asked:
What does Jim have *on* his desk? Do you *walk* to school?
Who sits *between* Linda and Peter? Pupils may reply as
follows: Jim has a pencil *on* his desk. Yes, I *walk* to school
every morning. Juanita sits *between* Linda and Peter.

e) The teacher may provide conversation and discussion
periods in which pupils are encouraged to use the new vocabulary and concepts learned. For example, after being
taught the word and concept of *water,* pupils may discuss
the importance of water to their daily lives, the various
forms of water, and the ways in which we utilize water. Such
a discussion period would do much in extending pupil understanding of the word and give the pupils opportunities to gain
verbal practice with the word.

f) After understanding of the word has been developed, pupils
should be given opportunities to read the word in various
contexts and situations. In the beginning, chart stories
developed with the pupils may be used. The children may
also write original stories individually, using the new word or
words learned. These stories may be shared orally and then
put into booklet form for the class to enjoy at their leisure.
The teacher should also place books in the classroom library
which feature the words and concepts studied.

g) The teacher should also provide experiences outside the
classroom to develop the children's concepts and vocabularies. Children may go on field trips by walking to places of
interest in the neighborhood or taking bus trips to more
distant places in the community where animals, objects, and
processes unfamiliar to the children may be observed. Trips
that may be of value in the immediate neighborhood include
walks to see changes in the season, homes or business es-
tablishments being built, soil erosion, a modern super-
market, operations of digging and lifting machines, or a
nearby fire station. Other places in the community that may
enrich the children's concepts and vocabulary include the
airport, post office, library, newspaper printing facilities,
bakery, harbor, police station, museum, aquarium, dairy,
factories, telephone exchange, and observatory. However, in
order for these first-hand experiences to be effective in
building concepts and vocabulary, the teacher must prepare
the children for the planned experience, connect vocabulary
and concepts to the experience, and utilize vocabulary and
concepts in discussion and writing after the experience. In
preliminary discussions of the trip to be taken, the teacher
should guide the children concerning important aspects of
the trip to be observed so that they may become critical ob-
servers of their environment. Discussions should be held

about what the children want to find out on the trip, what they might want to ask their guide, and what they should look for. Following the field trip, the teacher should guide the children in evaluating the extent to which the purposes of the trip were achieved. They might discuss whether they accomplished what they set out to do, whether they found the answers to their questions, and what information they gained.

Development of Grammar

1. The audiolingual approach is an effective means for helping bilingual children learn the grammatical (including syntactical and morphological) elements of standard English. This approach is a speaker-hearer process and the step-by-step procedure for teaching grammatical elements is as follows:
   a) The teacher produces the structure model and repeats it several times.
   b) The teacher provides the cues, with the whole class, small groups, and then individuals responding to the cues.
   c) The pupils are given opportunities to use the specific structure models taught independently in a variety of situations.

2. Tape record some of the children's favorite stories to familiarize them with the syntactical regularities of standard English. If there are filmstrips available for the stories, they may be viewed as the recording is played.

3. The teacher may verbalize some of the children's first-hand experiences. Then he may record stories of the experiences for individual listening. The stories may also be duplicated in the form of a booklet, with blank pages included for the children's own illustrations. The illustrations may serve as contextual clues as the pupils read the story individually or to each other. These story booklets may be taken home by the children who may read the stories to their parents or have the stories read to them by their parents.

4. Have each child make sets of cards with words and phrases that form sentences. Use different colored paper for each sentence so that the cards will not be placed in the wrong sets. When the cards are not in use, put a rubber band around each set to keep the sets separate. When the color of a set is called, the pupils are to arrange the words and phrases to form a sentence which best expresses the thought. Ask the pupil who completes the task first to read his sentence to the class. If his sentence arrangement is not the best, call on another pupil to read his arrangement. Continue this procedure until the best one is read. Then have the whole class read the sentence orally. For example, one set of cards may contain the following words and phrases: that present, bought, Ellen, for you. The children may arrange the cards in these ways: a) That present Ellen bought for you; b) Ellen bought for

you that present; c) Ellen bought that present for you. The pupils who placed the cards in the last arrangement would have selected the best sentence.

5. Write on the chalkboard a list of words which belong in different word classes. Then read various incomplete sentences to the pupils with words omitted in different parts of the sentences. Ask the pupils to select the word from the chalkboard list which best completes each sentence. For example, words listed may include: *biggest, walks, quietly, for.* Incomplete sentences read by the teacher may include:

    a) Jack _____ to school everyday.

    b) I bought this ice cream cone _____ you.

    c) He ate the _____ piece of pie.

    d) Maria spoke _____ because her baby sister was sleeping.

If he wishes to do so, the teacher may write the words on small cards and the sentences on durable paper so that the children may do this exercise as an independent activity.

6. The teacher should continually evaluate the needs of the children in terms of the grammatical aspects of standard English. He may devise lessons on tape to provide practice with structural patterns that are causing children difficulty. Each lesson should focus on one item of difficulty. Each item selected for correction and practice should be called to the attention of the children and discussed with them to enable them to become aware of the differences between the pattern they use and the pattern used in standard English. The lesson should help the children learn to discriminate between the two patterns and give them oral practice with the structural pattern being taught. The recording should give the pupils opportunity to repeat the structural pattern after it has been heard. After initial introduction and instruction by the teacher of a particular structural pattern, the taped lessons may be used for independent practice.

7. The Language Master may also be used to provide practice with structural patterns of standard English. The machine records and plays back from a strip of recording tape which is fastened to a card. The cards may be purchased for a nominal cost in sets of 100. Thus, it is possible for the teacher to develop a program to meet the particular needs of his children. The machine has a two track audio system so the child may listen to a structural pattern prerecorded by the teacher, record his reproduction of the same pattern, listen to it, and then compare it with the teacher's if he wishes to evaluate what he has recorded.

8. A buddy or tutorial system may be utilized whereby pupil pairs drill and teach each other. Pairs may have similar needs, or a bilingual child may be paired with a standard English-speaking child. Pairs may consist of pupils within the same classroom or grade level or be from

different grade levels. Pupil pairs may be used not only for structural pattern practice but also for phonological and vocabulary practice.

9. After observation of the children's needs, the teacher may develop a wall chart which shows standard and nonstandard equivalents for the aspects of the English language with which the children seem to be having the most difficulty.

10. Have the children engage in substitution drills, replacement drills, cued-answer drills, transformation drills, and pattern drills in order to provide practice with the standard English dialect *(22)*.

Substitution Drills.
    Peter's going to school. He's going to school.
    Judy's going to school. She's going to school.
    Use sentence structures which have already been taught.

Replacement Drills.
    Teacher: Henry threw the ball. (T points to *caught.*)
    Students: Henry caught the ball.
    Teacher: Henry caught the ball. (T points to *he.*)
    Students: He caught the ball.

Write the replacement items on the chalkboard *(caught, he)*. After the sentence is presented, point to one of the words and have the pupils replace the equivalent in the sentence.

Cued-Answer Drills. Ask questions which require specific individual or group responses.
    Teacher: Where did Bob go?
    Students: He went to the park.

Transformation Drills. Present sentences for the pupils to transform.
    Teacher: Billy likes to read.
    Students: Does Billy like to read?
    Teacher: Rabbits eat carrots.
    Students: Carrots are eaten by rabbits.

Pattern Drills. In teaching the basic sentence structures, have the pupils compose their own sentences using the same basic pattern taught.
    Children play. Boys run. Girls skip.
    She is happy. We are sad. They are tired.

11. Have the children translate statements from their first language to standard English. Discuss the differences in the statement which convey the same meaning and the various situations when the statements may be appropriately used.
    Nonstandard: I no go home now.
    Standard: I'm not going home now.

Oral Language Development

The children should engage in as many oral language activities as possible in the classroom in order to be able to gain practice with the standard English skills being taught. It is only through this means that standard English will be internalized within the bilingual child. The teacher should find numerous occasions in the course of a school day to provide the child with such oral language situations as conversation; discussion; storytelling; telephoning; dramatization; reporting; giving announcements, directions, and explanations; and choral speaking.

1. *Conversation.* When conversations are first carried on in the classroom under the guidance of the teacher, the main purpose should be to help children feel comfortable and create within them the desire and the willingness to engage in the conversations. The hesitancy, the fear of expressing themselves orally, must disappear and be replaced with feelings of confidence and enjoyment in participation. This can best be accomplished by permitting the children to use whichever language they are most comfortable with when conversing with their peers. The conversation groups should be kept small (two to four pupils per group) so as many pupils as possible will be able to participate in the conversations. In or out of school experiences may be selected as topics of conversation. Suggestions for the children to talk about might include favorite television programs, sports activities, games they enjoy playing, family or peer activities at home, foods they like or dislike, things they enjoy doing most, pets, recent books read, and motion picture films seen. The teacher should move inconspicuously about the room as the pupils converse with one another and observe the language or dialect being used and note specific linguistic needs.

When the children have reached the point where they are able to converse naturally and spontaneously about matters of common interest, the teacher might gradually guide the children in improving their quality of expression, help them recognize the areas in which they need improvement, provide separate language lessons to meet those needs, and encourage them to follow through in using the skills taught during conversation periods. In addition to specific linguistic needs, certain skills which need to be developed for effective conversation include adhering to the subject, using a variety of sentence constructions, using pleasing and descriptive vocabulary, enunciating clearly, knowing when it is and is not appropriate to talk, being sensitive to the feelings of others by speaking in a pleasant and interesting tone of voice, and being able to tactfully change the topic of conversation.

2. *Discussion.* Discussion is the form of oral expression used most frequently in the classroom for carrying on learning. It is a means for children to gain information, deal with facts and solve problems, express ideas and opinions, and share knowledge. Discussion also

provides opportunities for children to interact with the adult language model, the teacher.

There are many occasions in the classroom when problems arise which need to be solved. The teacher should guide the pupils in seeing a problem clearly so they can work toward its solution. As the pupils progress through the grades, they should assume greater responsibility for defining and setting up the problem to be solved. In order to gain as much pupil participation in discussions as possible, the topic being discussed should be one that is real and meaningful and has a purpose which is clear to each pupil. The topic should be of interest to the children and be within the range of their experiences; they should be made aware of the importance of the problem. Early in the school year, it would be helpful to discuss problems which would be followed by action so that bilingual pupils could see their ideas and suggestions applied in solving problems. Such activities as planning a program for parents, planning a classroom party, or publishing a classroom or school newspaper would necessitate many discussions for achieving the children's goals.

In guiding discussions, the teacher should avoid critical comments about the children's speech. If the children should make nonstandard statements and the opportunity arises, the teacher might repeat the statements in standard English in a casual manner as part of the discussion. If necessary, separate language lessons should be given to help the children in their areas of linguistic needs. Other skills to be developed in relation to discussions include staying on the topic being discussed, expressing disagreement in a tactful manner, forming independent judgments on the information available, making worthwhile contributions which are supported by facts, raising questions that are pertinent and asking for explanations freely, avoiding repetition of what has been said through careful listening, taking turns in speaking, and listening courteously while others speak.

3. *Storytelling.* Storytelling is a means for children to share personal experiences and stories they have read or heard.

Before children are able to effectively tell stories in standard English so that others may enjoy them, they must have many experiences in listening to stories, reading a variety of books, and doing things and going to places of interest. Bilingual children may be lacking in experiences in these areas, so it is especially important that the teacher of such children provide them with suitable activities to fill the void.

With bilingual children, it probably would be best to have them begin by telling stories of their personal experiences at school or at home. For example, following a field trip by the class, each pupil might tell about what he considered to be the most interesting part of the trip. Each pupil's contribution could be taped and later typewritten and put together in booklet form. Later, when the children are confident and find enjoyment in sharing their experiences, they may be encouraged to share stories they've enjoyed reading, hearing, or creating. To stimulate interest in storytelling, children may be encouraged to pantomime or act out portions of a story to be told. Hand or stick puppets, flannelboard figures, or a motion picture "film" made by the pupils may be used in the storytelling presentation. Children who have read or heard the same story may get together to plan and carry out a storytelling presentation.

To provide practice in meeting linguistic needs in standard English, children may be encouraged to use some of the structural patterns taught. However, this should not be done at the expense of making the children feel stilted and uncomfortable in their expression. Other storytelling skills and abilities that may be developed include enunciating clearly; expressing ideas in sequence and using voice to convey mood and meaning; speaking in a poised, natural, and animated manner; enriching vocabulary by using new words and meanings; and learning to appreciate and enjoy the experiences and original thoughts of others.

4. *Telephoning.* Learning to use a telephone properly is a skill which should be developed because of the importance of the telephone as a medium of communication in everyday life. Children may use the telephone to converse with friends and relatives; to call the police, fire department, or doctor in emergencies; or to receive messages for other members of the family.

The use of a toy or model telephone to carry on typical imaginary conversations is an excellent means to stimulate bilingual children to forget their shyness and self-consciousness and express themselves spontaneously and freely. After the children have gained confidence in expressing themselves, the class may evaluate the good and poor points of the calls made, suggest how they could be improved, and then apply suggestions made in further dramatizations of telephone calls. The children may follow up on what they learn in school by making calls at home and reporting their experiences to the class.

Skills and attitudes to be developed in teaching the use of the telephone include speaking clearly and distinctly in a pleasant tone of voice; formulating concisely the message, inquiry, or order before making the call; identifying oneself clearly and courteously when making or answering a call; stating clearly and courteously the purpose of the call; and allowing the caller to close the conversation. Additional telephoning techniques that should be learned are how to make long distance and emergency calls, how to get the operator, and how to use different sections of the directory to quickly find numbers.

5. *Dramatization.* Children seem to have an innate tendency to dramatize. In early childhood they love to imitate older people and

their activities. Through such activities, children identify with other people and interpret their actions. In so doing, they further their learning of language by experimenting with new words, new ideas, and new ways of doing and saying things. They gain richer and deeper understandings of the world about them; experiences in using their imaginations and creative abilities; and greater facilities in expressing feelings, in phrasing and ordering sentences, and in using more vivid and expressive speaking vocabularies. By observing the spontaneous dramatic activities of preschool or elementary age children, the teacher is able to gain a better knowledge of past experiences of the children and of their understandings, skills, and attitudes.

Because bilingual children may be less verbal in dramatic situations, the teacher may need to participate actively by playing various roles and making comments which will stimulate more oral expression by the children. For example, in a particular situation, the children may be preparing a meal with no one doing any speaking. The teacher might then knock on the door and be an unexpected guest at the home. As a guest at the meal, he might comment on the delicious food and ask questions about who prepared the meal and about some of the current activities of the members of the family in the play situation. As the children begin to express themselves more freely, the teacher should participate less and less in the dramatic activities. Stick puppets, hand puppets, and flannelboard figures may also be used in the dramatizations to help bilingual children become less self-conscious and freer to express themselves.

As the children grow older and gain more interests and experiences, the dramatization they engage in is likely to become more complex. There is a steady progression from individual, spontaneous play to planned and more organized group play. They will seek new facts, information, and materials to enrich their dramatizations and gain new relationships and new understandings.

Skills to be developed in dramatic activities include speaking clearly and expressively, speaking with sufficient volume to be easily heard by the audience, working cooperatively with others in achieving a common goal, showing consideration and appreciation for the ideas and needs of others, using words effectively and correctly in various structural patterns, and feeling the part of the portrayed character and employing his tone and mood.

6. *Reporting.* Reporting on various topics of personal interest and concern is an excellent means for bilingual children to practice standard English skills learned. In the primary grades, oral reports are given informally and spontaneously by the children as they share information or knowledge gained through personal or vicarious experiences. As the children progress through the middle and upper elementary grades, they should learn how to give planned reports.

Such reports may be about books or stories they've enjoyed reading, individual or group science experiments, committee work, social studies or science topics of interest, or trips taken with the family. For these reports, the children should select and organize information according to the purpose of the report and include some of their own interpretations of the ideas gained. To help children adhere to the topics of their reports, be sure they have specific questions in mind which the reports are to answer. A child who is to give an oral report in class should be led to feel that he is making an important contribution to the group. The tape recorder may be used for practice and self-evaluation under the guidance of the teacher before actual presentation of the report to the class.

If a child seems to be generally disinterested in school activities but seems to have a strong interest in a particular topic, the teacher may encourage him to gather information on the topic and share it with his classmates with an oral report accompanied by appropriate visual aids done by the child. A project of this kind can give the child the recognition he needs, help him feel an important part of the group, and stimulate his interest in other school activities.

Skills that children should develop through planning and giving an oral report include selecting a specific topic, problem, or question they want to know more about; presenting the report in an interesting way by using charts, pictures, books, diagrams, and other visual materials; keeping the topic in mind as they gather information; telling the facts in good order so that the report is meaningful and can be fully comprehended by classmates; speaking distinctly and expressively in good sentence form; and evaluating the report in terms of its interest, organization, choice of words and sentence structures, and usefulness to the group.

7. *Giving announcements, directions, and explanations.* Children frequently find the need to make announcements and give directions and explanations in their school and life situations throughout the day. Announcements are made by children about school or class programs, lost and found items, meetings, games, or exhibits. Children find the need to give directions or explanations for playing games, constructing various projects, putting on a play, or telling how a particular event occurred. Bilingual children will profit from practice in giving announcements, directions, and explanations as they will learn the importance of selecting appropriate words and sentence patterns to convey exactly what they want to communicate.

The skills which the children need to develop for making announcements and giving directions and explanations effectively include organizing ideas clearly and concisely; providing all essential information as to who, what, when, where, and how; using appropriate vocabulary and sentence structure; speaking distinctly so that everyone can hear easily; and repeating for emphasis important information regarding what, where, and when.

8. *Choral speaking.* In working with bilingual children, the teacher may find a number who are generally hesitant in expressing themselves orally. The use of choral speaking is an excellent way to help children gradually to become relaxed and comfortable in speaking before others. It will also help such children develop their knowledge and skills concerning the phonological and grammatical aspects of standard English. Specific speaking skills that the teacher should help the children develop are clear enunciation and correct pronunciation, rich and full tonal quality, and flexibility. Choral speaking also helps children enjoy the rhythm, mood, and meaning of poetry and prose; teaches children to listen and think creatively as they interpret words and word patterns; and encourages the understanding, memorization, and appreciation of children's literature.

Children who have had rich and varied experiences in listening to literature read by the teacher will readily and enthusiastically participate in choral speaking. In the preschool and primary grade years, children enjoy joining the teacher in saying rhyming and repetitive phrases or sentences of stories, poems, and nursery rhymes. From this background, the children can be led easily into actual choral speaking.

Techniques that will help to make the choral speaking experiences enjoyable and worthwhile include the following:
   a) Choose material carefully, considering such factors as the interests and intellectual and emotional levels of the children and selecting only those poems which have rhythm, a universal theme or group sentiment, and literary value.
   b) Interpret the poem fully so children grasp its mood and meaning and discuss such questions as: What is the poem about? Does it make you feel happy, sad, excited? What pictures do you see in your mind? What sounds or descriptive words are used to make pictures? What part is the most exciting or interesting? Which of your five senses are appealed to and how? Why do you think the poem was written?
   c) Discuss various ways in which the poem may be said. Which lines should be said quickly or slowly? Softly or loudly? Which parts should be said by all voices? By a few voices? By light voices? By heavy voices? By medium voices? Arrangements using different voice qualities would probably not be possible until the upper elementary grades. After discussing and trying various arrangements, both teacher and children may evaluate their efforts and make suggestions for varying or improving the arrangements until they are satisfied with the outcome. Then the children may repeat the selection for pleasure *(21)*.

The following types of arrangement may be used in the choral speaking of a selection *(1):*
  a) Refrain. A child reads the narrative, with the whole class joining in on the refrain.
  b) Antiphonal or two part. Two balanced groups are used, one against the other—boys versus girls, light voices versus heavy voices.
  c) Sequential or line-a-child. A few individuals interpet a line or two at a time, leading up to a climax with the whole class joining in.
  d) Part arrangement. Voices of various types of quality are grouped as in a singing choir.
  e) Unison. All voices are used to speak all lines at the same time.

If bilingual children are to communicate their ideas and feelings to others in their everyday life and if they are to succeed in learning to read standard English, they must learn to speak effectively in standard English. Therefore, the teacher of such children must be aware of the oral language skills he must help the children develop, and he must provide frequent and continuous opportunities for oral expression.

Chapter 4

FORMAL READING INSTRUCTION

The bilingual child is ready for formal reading instruction only when he has acquired adequate oral language, vocabulary, concept development, and other prerequisites of reading skills. At this stage, what approach or approaches might be effective in his reading instruction?

The teacher of bilingual children must recognize the fact that no one particular reading approach or single combination of approaches will guarantee that the bilingual child will learn to read. The teacher must be knowledgeable concerning a variety of reading approaches and procedures that will enable him to select and utilize effectively the approach or approaches that will best meet the needs of the bilingual children. The teacher must also realize that, as certain needs are met, it may be necessary to change the reading approach to meet other needs.

● **Some Factors to Consider in Selecting Reading Approaches**

1. *Linking oral language and reading.* If the children are lacking in reading experiences at home, the teacher may find the language experience approach an effective one in launching the children into formal reading. In this approach, the children dictate from their own experiences those things of interest to them and which they may wish to share with others. The teacher writes down what the children relate and they see that what they say is important and can be written down and eventually read. Thus, the content of what the children read represents concepts that are part of their culture and are meaningful and important to them. This approach implements some of the linguistic principles that are important in second language teaching *(17)*:

   a) Items should be presented in spoken form before they are presented in written form.
   b) Content should stimulate real-life situations and relate as closely as possible to the sociocultural background of the child.
   c) Language is something you understand and say before it is something you read and write.

The language experience approach has a number of advantages for the bilingual child:

a) Self-concept. This is a highly personal, individualized approach. Thus, it can build positive relationships between teacher and pupil and can help the child see that he is an important individual in the eyes of his teacher.

b) Language arts interrelated. As previously stated, this approach helps the child see the interrelationships among the language arts. He easily sees that: What I can think about, I can say. What I can say, I can write. What I can write, I can read. I can read what I can write and what others have written for me to read (15). In other words, the child sees that reading is nothing more than talk written down.

c) Meaningful content. Too often when the bilingual child begins learning to read, he is thrust into reading materials with content that he cannot relate to or that has no meaning for him. This results in lack of motivation to read on the part of the child. When the language experience approach is used, since the content *is* the child's actual experiences which have been of interest to him, what he reads is certain to be meaningful and stimulating.

The language experience approach also has its limitations when used with the bilingual child:

a) Vocabulary control difficult. Because the sentences are the child's own contributions, it is often difficult for the teacher to control the vocabulary load of the stories and there may not be enough repetition of words to have the child build his repertoire of sight words.

b) Limited content. In this approach, the child's reading experiences would be limited to the experiential and informational backgrounds of himself and his peers unless the teacher encourages and makes available the use of other sources of reading material.

c) Reinforcement of unacceptable forms of speech. Because the stories read by the bilingual child are his own words and structural patterns, grossly unacceptable forms of speech may be reinforced. In using this approach with the bilingual child, the challenge lies in the teacher's ability to encourage the child to express himself freely and to teach him to make use of standard forms; at the same time, he must be certain not to deprecate the child's first language and social and cultural backgrounds. A sympathetic and compassionate teacher should be able to achieve this with little difficulty. If the child contributes a nonstandard pattern for his story, the teacher might accept and value the child's idea with positive comments on the idea and then tactfully suggest possible alternatives in standard form. If unacceptable forms of English are reinforced through writing, we will be increasing the burden for the child in his efforts to learn standard English forms.

Books that should aid the teacher in the use of the language experience approach are: *Learning to Read through Experience (15)*, *Teaching Reading as a Language Experience (10)*, and *The Language Experience Approach to the Teaching of Reading (26)*. These books offer many suggestions for stimulating oral expression, planning for skill development, keeping records, and evaluating reading development.

Language Experiences in Reading (2), a kit of resource materials which includes a teacher's guide, daily lesson plans, filmstrips, reading selections, story starters, recorded songs, listening activities, and decoding materials, provides the teacher with additional practical help in the use of the language experience approach. The authors of the kit also offer three sets of teacher training filmstrips and cassettes to be used with the language experience resource materials.

2. *Sequential development of reading skills.* It is especially important for the teacher to help bilingual children acquire the basic reading skills that will make it possible for them to succeed in learning to read and to gain independence in reading. Areas of skill development should include vocabulary (word meaning) skills; word recognition skills, including contextual, phonetic, and structural analyses; comprehension skills, including critical reading skills.

Which reading approach or approaches may prove to be most effective in developing these skills? A basal reading approach will probably provide the teacher with the most guidance and help in developing these skills. However, the series selected for use with the children must be chosen with care and a number of important factors must be considered:

    a) Content should be relevant and meaningful for the children with whom it is to be used. The most relevant materials for bilingual children are those which communicate in their content that the people of each ethnic group—Black, Mexican-American, Chinese-American—are respectable, contributing citizens and real human beings capable of love, hate, fear, disappointment, anger, success, and achievement whether they are pictured in a ghetto, a classroom, suburbia, or rural areas of America *(31)*.

    b) Phonological and structural patterns used in the content should be within the children's speech repertoire.

    c) Vocabulary control should not be so rigid as to stultify content and destroy the children's interest in reading.

    d) A variety of exercises and activities should be provided for meeting the needs of the children in the development of their basic reading skills and for extending their reading experiences.

A number of basal reading series offer materials concerned with the various ethnic and racial groups in both urban and suburban settings. They include the Macmillan Bank Street Readers, the Webster Skyline Series, the Follett Great Cities Reading Improvement Program, and the Scott, Foresman series, Open Highways. Current basal series offer science materials, stories with masculine appeal in a variety of family and environmental settings, and stories drawn from good children's literature (25). Whichever basal series the teacher chooses to use to meet the needs of his children, it is important for him to use these materials creatively and selectively as a guide and aid in his teaching of reading rather than rigidly in stereotyped, consecutive order.

A reading series which was designed especially for bilingual children (English and Spanish languages) is the Miami Linguistic Reader Series by D. C. Heath. In these linguistic readers, one primary emphasis is to teach the child to correctly pronounce the English language. Much practice is given on discriminating minimal pairs and enunciation of all the English phonemes that are not in the Spanish language. Throughout the series aural-oral mastery of the material that is to be read is emphasized. The series is based on the following linguistic, as well as pedagogical, premises and should aid the teacher in his reading instruction of children who speak Spanish as a first language (37):

a) The referential content of beginning reading material must deal with those things which time has shown are interesting to children.

b) The materials must reflect the natural language forms of children's speech.

c) The child must have aural-oral control of the material he is expected to read.

d) The focus must be on the process of reading as a thinking process rather than on the uses of reading after decoding has been mastered.

e) Sound-symbol correspondence (phoneme-grapheme relationships) in beginning reading should be in terms of spelling patterns rather than in terms of individual letter-sound correspondences.

f) Grammatical structure and vocabulary must be controlled.

g) Children must learn to read by structures if they are to master the skills involved in the act of reading.

h) The learning load in linguistically oriented materials must be determined in terms of the special nature of the materials.

i) Writing experiences reinforce listening, speaking, and reading.

j) Materials must be sequenced so that they enable the learner to achieve success as he progresses through the materials.

The Miami Linguistic Readers have proved to be very effective with bilingual children when used by creative teachers.Other linguistically oriented materials that may be used in the instruction of bilingual children include *Let's Read* by Leonard Bloomfield and Clarence Barnhart, Wayne State University Press; *Linguistic Readers* by Henry Lee Smith, Jr., et al., Benziger Corporation; *Merrill Linguistic Readers* by Charles C. Fries, et al., Charles E. Merrill; *Basic Reading Series* by Lynn Goldberg and Donald Rasmussen, Science Research Associates; *Sound and Letters Series* by Frances Adkins Halls, Linguistic; and *Structural Reading Series* by Catherine Stern, L. W. Singer. Generally, most of these texts present a carefully controlled vocabulary. The words introduced stress a particular group of sounds of high consistency in the manner in which they are spelled. Thus, a number of words containing the *at* spelling are presented, followed by another group containing the *an* spelling, and so forth. For the most part, each group of words with common phonemes is composed of monosyllables; for example, *mat, sat, hat* and *can, ran, fan.* A second group of words varies only in vowel pattern; for example, *hat, hit* and *tan, ten.* The progression continues from three to four letter words, from regular to irregular words, and finally to polysyllabic words *(25).*

3. *Broadening reading experiences and stimulating recreational reading.* It is important for the bilingual child to develop a positive attitude toward reading so that he will read for pleasure during his free time in school or at home. A variety of approaches may be used to stimulate the child to do independent reading and broaden his reading experiences. These include listening centers that expose children to good books, a film viewing center with filmstrips relating to good stories in children's literature, an attractive library area filled with good books on the children's reading levels, a regular storytelling time by teacher and pupils, individual or group projects on stories read and enjoyed, individual record keeping of books read by children, panel discussions on books read, and book ownership through joining children's book clubs.

Individualized reading is one of the most effective reading approaches for developing a positive attitude toward reading and stimulating independent reading on the part of children. After the child has developed a basic sight vocabulary and has sufficient reading skills for some degree of independence in reading, the teacher might utilize this approach along with the others being used in the classroom.

The individualized reading approach is one in which the child is self-seeking and self-pacing. He has the opportunity to select the book he wishes to read from a classroom library which has shelves of interesting books. This approach provides many opportunities for interpersonal relationships between teacher and pupil and among the pupils themselves. There are also opportunities for creative expression and the development of basic reading skills.

Books that should be particularly helpful to the teacher in the use of the individualized reading approach are: *Individualizing Your Reading Program (29), Educator's Guide to Personalized Reading Instruction (5),* and *Individualizing Reading Practices (12).* These books offer many suggestions for the initial organizational steps in implementing this approach, individual conferencing, planning follow-up activities, record keeping, skill development, and other essential elements of the individualized approach to the teaching of reading.

● **Conclusion**

Teaching reading to the bilingual child does not differ from teaching reading to the monolingual child, if the child is first helped to learn the phonemic and grammatical elements of English that differ from his first language before he is expected to learn to read English. Essentially needed is a teacher who understands, appreciates, and respects the cultural background of the child; who knows the phonemic and grammatical differences between standard English and the child's first language so that he can help the child with his linguistic needs; and who is knowledgeable concerning the various reading approaches so that he will be able to select and utilize those approaches that best meet the particular needs of the bilingual child.

References

1. Abney, Louise. "Poetry: Interpretation," *Guides to Speech Training in the Elementary School,* a report of the Elementary Committee of the National Association of Teachers of Speech. Boston: Expression Company, 1943.

2. Allen, Roach Van, and Claryce Allen. *Language Experiences in Reading.* Chicago: Encyclopedia Britannica, 1975.

3. Allen, Roach Van, and Claryce Allen. *Teacher Training Materials for LEIR.* Chicago: Encyclopedia Britannica, 1975.

4. Arnold, Richard D. *1965–1966 Year Two Findings, San Antonio Language Research Project.* Austin: University of Texas, 1968.

5. Barbe, Walter B. *Educator's Guide to Personalized Reading Instruction.* Englewood Cliffs, New Jersey: Prentice-Hall, 1961.

6. Baratz, Joan C., and Roger W. Shuy (Eds.). *Teaching Black Children to Read.* Washington, D.C.: Center for Applied Linguistics, 1969.

7. Edwards, Thomas J. "Learning Problems in Cultural Deprivation," in J. Allen Figurel (Ed.), *Reading and Inquiry,* Convention Proceedings. Newark, Delaware: International Reading Association, 1965, 256–261.

8. Eisenberg, Leon, et al. "Class and Race Effects on the Intelligibility of Monosyllables," *Child Development,* 1968, 1077–1089.

9. Goodman, Kenneth S. "Dialect Barriers to Reading Comprehension," *Elementary English,* December 1965, 853–860.

10. Hall, MaryAnne. *Teaching Reading as a Language Experience.* Columbus, Ohio: Charles E. Merrill, 1970.

11. Horn, Thomas D., and Richard D. Arnold. "Capsule Description of San Antonio Language Bilingual Research Project," University of Texas at Austin, 1967, mimeographed.

12. Jacobs, Leland, et al. *Individualizing Reading Practices.* New York: Bureau of Publications, Teachers College, Columbia University, 1958.

13. Knight, Lester N. *Language Arts for the Exceptional: The Gifted and the Linguistically Different.* Itasca, Illinois: F. E. Peacock, 1974, 106–107.

14. Labov, William. "Some Sources of Reading Problems for Negro Speakers of Nonstandard English," *New Directions in Elementary English.* Urbana, Illinois: National Council of Teachers of English, 1967, 140–167.

15. Lee, Dorris M., and Roach Van Allen. *Learning to Read through Experience.* New York: Appleton-Century-Crofts, 1963, 5–7.

16. Modiano, Nancy. "National or Mother Language in Beginning Reading: A Comparative Study," *Research in the Teaching of English,* 1968, 32–43.

17. O'Brien Carmen A. *Teaching the Language Different Child to Read.* Columbus, Ohio: Charles E. Merrill, 1973, 104.

18. Orata, Pedro T. "The Iloilo Community School Experiment: The Vernacular as Medium of Instruction," *Fundamental and Adult Education,* 1956, 173–178.

19. Orata, Pedro T. "The Iloilo Experiment in Education through the Vernacular," *Progressive Education,* April 1953, 185–189.

20. Peisach, E. Cherry. "Children's Comprehension of Teacher and Peer Speech," *Child Development,* 1965, 467–480.

21. Raubicheck, Letitia. *Choral Speaking is Fun.* New York: Noble and Noble, 1955, 7–9.

22. Ruddell, Robert B. *Reading-Language Instruction: Innovative Practices.* Englewood Cliffs, New Jersey: Prentice-Hall, 1974, 275, 278, 283–284.

23. Shuy, Roger W. " A Linguistic Background for Developing Beginning Reading Materials for Black Children," in Joan Baratz and Roger Shuy (Eds.), *Teaching Black Children to Read.* Washington, D.C.: Center for Applied Linguistics, 1969, 117–137.

24. Smith, Donald Hugh. "A Speaker Model Project to Enhance Pupils' Self-Esteem," *Journal of Negro Education,* Spring 1967, 177–180.

25. Spache, George, and Evelyn Spache. *Reading in the Elementary School.* Boston: Allyn and Bacon, 1973, 183, 222–223.

26. Stauffer, Russell G. *The Language Experience Approach to the Teaching of Reading.* New York: Harper and Row, 1970.

27. Stewart, William A. "On the Use of Negro Dialect in the Teaching of Reading," in Joan Baratz and Roger Shuy (Eds.), *Teaching Black Children to Read.* Washington, D.C.: Center for Applied Linguistics, 1969, 156–219.

28. Tireman, Lloyd S. "A Study of Fourth Grade Reading Vocabulary of Native Spanish Speaking Children," *Elementary School Journal,* December 1945, 223–227.

29. Veatch, Jeannette. *Individualizing Your Reading Program.* New York: G. P. Putnam's Sons, 1959.

30. Venezky, Richard L. "Nonstandard Language and Reading," *Elementary English,* March 1970, 334–345.

31. Vick, Marian L. "Relevant Content for the Black Elementary School Pupil," in Jerry L. Johns (Ed.), *Literacy for Diverse Learners.* Newark, Delaware: International Reading Association, 1974, 20–21.

32. Weener, Paul D. "Social Dialect Differences and the Recall of Verbal Messages," *Journal of Educational Psychology,* 1969, 194–199.

33. Weinrich, Uriel. *Languages in Contact: Findings and Problems.* New York: Linguistic Circle of New York, 1953, 1–2.

34. Welty, Stella Liu. "Reading and Black English," in Carl Braun (Ed.), *Language, Reading, and the Communication Process.* Newark, Delaware: International Reading Association, 1971, 71-93.

35. Wolfram, Walter A. *A Sociolinguistic Description of Detroit Negro Speech.* Washington, D.C.: Center for Applied Linguistics, 1969.

36. Wolfram, Walter A., and Ralph W. Fasold. "Toward Reading Materials for Speakers of Black English: Three Linguistically Appropriate Passages," in Joan Baratz and Roger Shuy (Eds.), *Teaching Black Children to Read.* Washington, D.C.: Center for Applied Linguistics, 1969, 138-155.

37. Zintz, Miles V. *The Reading Process: The Teacher and the Learner.* Dubuque, Iowa: William C. Brown, 1970, 326, 333.